W9-DEW-099

The Little Book of Hockey Sweaters

Andrew Podnieks and Rob Hynes

Illustrated by Anthony Jenkins

KEY PORTER BOOKS

Text copyright © 2005 by Andrew Podnieks and Rob Hynes
Illustration copyright © 2005 by Anthony Jenkins

All rights reserved. No part of this work covered by the copyrights hereon may be reproduced or used in any form or by any means—graphic, electronic or mechanical, including photocopying, recording, taping or information storage and retrieval systems—without the prior written permission of the publisher, or, in case of photocopying or other reprographic copying, a licence from Access Copyright, the Canadian Copyright Licensing Agency, One Yonge Street, Suite 1900, Toronto, Ontario, M6B 3A9.

Library and Archives Canada Cataloguing in Publication

Podnieks, Andrew
    The little book of hockey sweaters / Andrew Podnieks ; illustrated by Anthony Jenkins.

ISBN 1-55263-716-6

    1. National Hockey League—Miscellanea. 2. Hockey—Miscellanea.
I. Title.

GV847.8.N3P58 2005   796.962'64   C2005-902746-0

The publisher gratefully acknowledges the support of the Canada Council for the Arts and the Ontario Arts Council for its publishing program. We acknowledge the support of the Government of Ontario through the Ontario Media Development Corporation's Ontario Book Initiative.

We acknowledge the financial support of the Government of Canada through the Book Publishing Industry Development Program (BPIDP) for our publishing activities.

Key Porter Books Limited
Six Adelaide Street East, Tenth Floor
Toronto, Ontario
Canada M5C 1H6

www.keyporter.com

Text design and layout: Ingrid Paulson

Printed and bound in Canada

05 06 07 08 09   5 4 3 2 1

Contents

Preface

ON THE SURFACE, this book may seem like a cute idea meant for trivia buffs: the minutiae of player identification by sweater number. But taken together these stories represent a league, a sport, and a culture. After reading these, you will see why particular numbers have a great deal of significance for hockey players. To some players, numbers are of minor importance, at best a superstitious or comforting digit. To others, though, the number makes the man: it is as essential to the spirit of the player as his childhood, his upbringing, or the skills that got him to the NHL. It is a numeric reminder of his past, his family, and his success. For many players, the story behind the wearing of a particular number is truly the most interesting aspect of his hockey character.

Perhaps no story is more extraordinary in its simplicity and importance than Robert Petrovicky's. He wore sweater 39— a bit odd, but not uncommonly so in this day and age. I had the opportunity to ask him why he wore that number. We were in Salt Lake City, February 2002, and he was playing for an undermanned Slovakia team at that year's Olympics. So there I was in the corridor outside the Slovak dressing room, talking to Petrovicky about his frustration at not having his team's best players. At the end, I asked him casually if there was any reason in particular why he wore 39. "Yes," he said. "That was how old my mother was when she was killed by a drunk driver."

At the other end of the spectrum, I phoned Eddie Shack one day and asked him why, during a career with so many teams, he always seemed to pick number 23 when it was available. "Because those are my initials backwards," he explained.

Somewhere in the middle are stories about well-known numbers, like the sacred 9 which became so after great players wore them—Gordie Howe, Maurice Richard, Bobby Hull—and which before were meaningless. As Gary Aldcorn observed, "you don't ask for a 9 unless you play like a 9."

Rob Hynes is the only guy I've met who is as obsessed with numbers as I am and not just for the statistical sake of memorizing who wore X with team Y in season Z. To be sure, Rob is a complete loon for remembering the aforementioned trivia, but he also likes to ask players for the story behind their number. He understands the subtext and realizes a sweater number is not a statistic so much as it is a biographical element in a player's life and career. Together, we have put together this collection of stories—funny, silly, profound—which works both superficially and historically as a testament to the players who have passed through the NHL. Many of these players are still active, some have retired, and a few have passed away, but their sweater number stories are as fascinating as any goal or assist they ever made in a game.

Andrew Podnieks
Toronto, September 2005

Gary Aldcorn

WHILE PLAYING midget hockey in Manitoba in the early 1950s, Gary Aldcorn and his team, the Winnipeg Monarchs, travelled to Dauphin for a tournament. It was there that he saw Don Marshall play. Marshall, captain of the Montreal Junior Canadiens, wore 19. Aldcorn thought the future Canadiens star was the same kind of player as he himself was, and in tribute, decided to wear 19 with the Monarchs. This worked out well for Aldcorn because he had wanted to have a nine in his number. "But," he explained, "you don't ask for a 9 unless you play like a 9, and you're not given a 9 unless you're a star." Thus, he paired a 1 with a 9 and kept the number when he made it to the Toronto Maple Leafs a few years later.

Glenn Anderson

WHEN IT CAME TO sweater numbers, Glenn Anderson got his way most of the time. His favourite number was always 9, the number he started his NHL career with in Edmonton back in 1980. It was also the number he wore with the Oilers for 11 years and the number he used while winning five Stanley Cups with the team. But when he was traded to Toronto at the start of the 1991–92 season, Dave Hannan already had 9, so Anderson went to the closest thing available, 10. Hannan left the team during the year to join Canada's National team, and Anderson took 9 the next training camp. He was traded to the Rangers at the deadline in early 1994, and again 9 was in use, this time by Adam Graves. So Anderson played a little numbers game by choosing 36 because 3 plus 6 equals 9. The next year in St. Louis and the year after that playing back in Edmonton, Anderson was able to wear his 9 again. During his final NHL season, 1995–96, he finished his playing days in St. Louis, this time having to go to 36 again as an alternate to 9, which was being used by Shayne Corson.

Mel Angelstad

BORN IN SASKATOON, Saskatchewan, on Hallowe'en 1972, Mel Angelstad was never drafted and made his way through the minor league ranks primarily as a tough guy. After a dozen seasons in the minors, he was called up to the Washington Capitals on April 3, 2004, as reward for such a long career in the minors, and for two games at the end of the 2003–04 season Angelstad could call himself an NHLer. More important, he made history by becoming the first player in the league to wear 69. "I asked for 68," he explained, because Jaromir Jagr, the team's previous 68, had been traded earlier in the season. "I thought I could fill his shoes," he deadpanned. "When they didn't give it to me, I decided to one-up Jags and chose 69." Angelstad ignored the sexual connotation of the number that had prevented any player in league history from wearing 69 previously. "When we played the Penguins," Angelstad recalled, "Richard Jackman was laughing and told me that number suited me. I played with him for two years in the Dallas system. As far as my teammates in Washington, they had a chuckle. Come to think of it, the number helped take away some of the butterflies you get playing your first NHL game."

Derek Armstrong

JOURNEYMAN CENTRE Derek Armstrong was drafted by the New York Islanders in 1992, moved on to Ottawa for a year and then settled with the New York Rangers in 1998, playing mostly in the minors for their farm team for three seasons. It was during his time on Broadway that Armstrong lived out a quirky little numbers history. In those three seasons, he played just seven games with the Blueshirts, but he managed to wear four different sweater numbers. In 1998–99 he played three games and wore 18. The following year, Armstrong was a late-season call-up for one game and found Mike York wearing 18, so he ended up with 37. In 2000–01, he went to training camp and was assigned 22, but after he failed to crack the team that number was assigned to defenceman Tomas Kloucek. Armstrong was recalled in January 2001, when he wore 17. When he was called up again later in the season, Colin Forbes was wearing 17, so Armstrong opted to wear 21. Interestingly, Armstrong wore 38 and 14 with the Islanders, and 42 as a member of the Ottawa Senators. He was traded to Los Angeles in 2002 and wore 32 in 2002–03 and 7 the next year. In all, Armstrong has used nine different sweater numbers in NHL play.

SUPERSTITION AND HOCKEY are strange bedfellows. Some players just don't feel like they can play their best if they don't have the number they want on their back. Donald Audette is such a player. When the Sabres traded him to the Los Angeles Kings in 1998, he was unable to wear 28 because it belonged to veteran defenceman Steve Duchesne. Another trade sent Audette to Atlanta, where he managed to reclaim his 28. The result was a career-high year in 2000–01. That summer, he signed with Dallas, where he also wore 28, but a trade to Montreal forced him to change numbers again. After a hot start with the Habs, wearing 22, Audette had his arm badly cut by a skate blade and the bulk of his season was wiped out. He blamed his bad luck on 22. "I've worn number 28 since junior," Audette said, "but since it belongs to Karl Dykhuis, I decided to take 82. Number 2 and number 8 have always been lucky for me." When he made his return to the Montreal lineup, Audette was wearing 82. In 12 playoff games, Audette recorded ten points, which tied him for the team scoring lead. That run proved to be his last hurrah. He struggled the next season and wound up in the minors.

Alex Auld

WHILE ALEX AULD is not a household name, he is linked to Vladislav Tretiak, the renowned Soviet goalie of the 1972 Summit Series. During his junior career with the North Bay Centennials (1997–2001), Auld wore 20 as a tribute to the Hall of Fame Soviet goaltender. The 2001–02 season was Auld's first year as a professional, and he appeared in one NHL game that year with Vancouver. Though the Canucks didn't give him 20—assigning him 35 instead—Auld's lucky number still played a role in his NHL debut. That first game was against the Dallas Stars with Ed Belfour in goal. Belfour has worn 20 for years in honour of Tretiak, his former goaltending coach. Auld commented on the significance of facing Belfour. "I met Eddie at the Tretiak goalie camp," he said. "Eddie wears 20 in honour of him [Tretiak] and I wore 20 in junior." Auld and the Canucks were able to defeat the Stars that night, 4–2. As luck would have it, Auld made 20 saves on the night.

DURING HIS YEARS as a goalie with the Chicago Blackhawks (1988–97), Ed Belfour found his familiar 30 unavailable when he was named to the Campbell Conference All-Star team in 1993 because veteran Mike Vernon was wearing the number. His solution was to wear 00. But that wasn't the only time Belfour made a number switch during his career. When he ended his very successful days in Chicago after being traded to San Jose in January 1997, the move also severed an important professional relationship for Belfour. His goaltending coach in Chicago was the great Soviet netminder Vladislav Tretiak, who wore 20 during a Hall of Fame career that saw him win ten gold medals at the World Championships. When Belfour joined the Sharks toward the end of the 1997–98 season, he decided to switch to 20 as a tribute to his former goalie coach and friend. When he moved to the Dallas Stars later that year, and then to the Toronto Maple Leafs in 2002, Belfour again wore 20. The tradition continues to this day as Belfour's son, Dayne, wears 20 as goalie for the Streetsville Derbys in the provincial junior hockey league in Toronto.

Jan Benda

THERE IS, PERHAPS, no more international player in the game today than Jan Benda, not well known in North America but a recognizable name in Europe. Born in Belgium, he played some junior hockey in southern Ontario and turned pro in Germany in 1992. He has represented Germany at several Olympics and World Championships, and played minor pro in North America, as well as nine games with the Washington Capitals in 1997–98. Benda wore 28 in the NHL simply because that number was given to him, but his international number, 83, has greater personal significance. Benda played in Prague for several years where he became good friends with Vladimir Ruzicka, who wore 83. Benda reversed that and wore 38 in the Czech league and he asked Ruzicka if he could wear 83 while representing Germany at the Worlds and Olympics. Ruzicka, honoured by his friend's gesture, consented. Ironically, Ruzicka wore 38 in the NHL with Boston (1990–93) and Ottawa (1993–94).

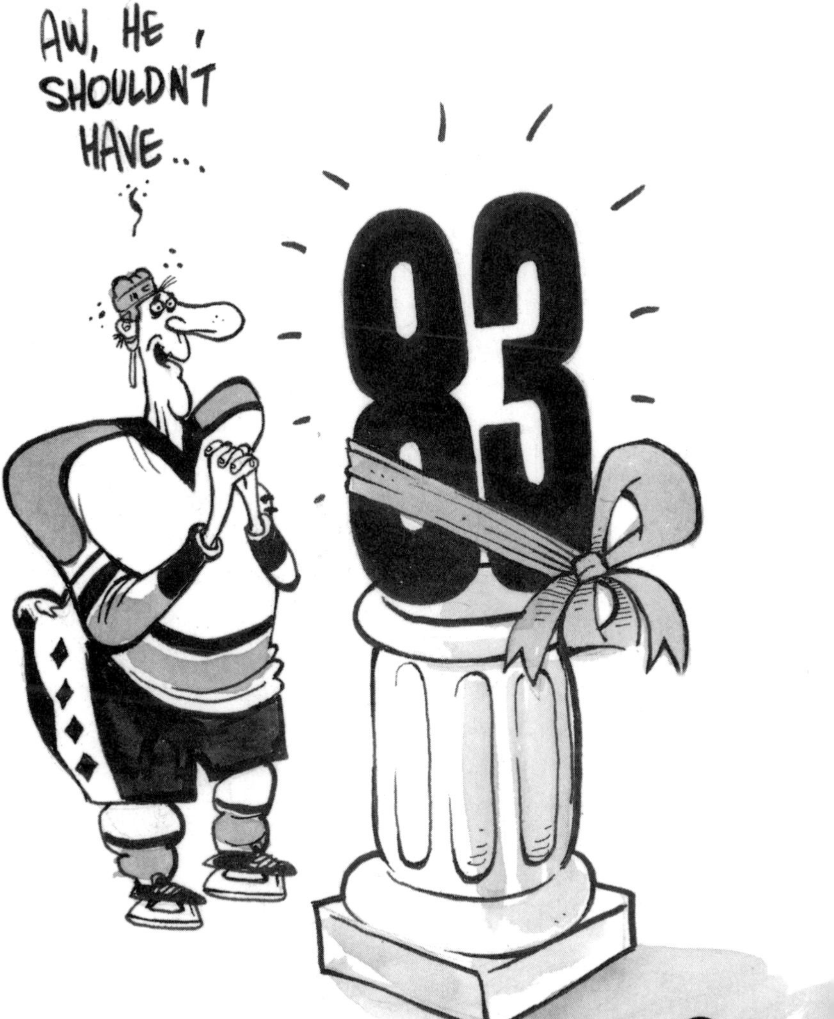
AW, HE SHOULDN'T HAVE...
83

IN THE SPAN OF just over a year, Patrice Bergeron made history for Team Canada. He was drafted by Boston 45th overall in 2003 and surprised everyone at the Bruins camp by making the NHL as an 18-year-old that fall. He had an excellent rookie season, scoring 16 goals, earning 39 points, and helping the team to the playoffs. After the team's first-round loss to Montreal, Bergeron was named to Team Canada for the 2004 World Championship in the Czech Republic. The two-way centre and a phenomenal faceoff man helped Canada win gold. With the NHL lockout cancelling the 2004–05 season, he joined Canada's junior team and led the team to gold again at the World Junior Championship in Grand Forks, North Dakota. He became the first player for any country to play at the senior World Championship *before* the World Juniors— and winning gold both times for good measure. He was given 37 when he got to Acadie-Bathurst in the Quebec Major Junior Hockey League (QMJHL) in 2002 and has continued to wear it everywhere he has played since.

Jason Bonsignore

A NATIVE OF ROCHESTER, New York, Jason Bonsignore played 79 games over four NHL seasons in the 1990s, always wearing the special and original 64 with Edmonton and Tampa Bay. His reasoning is simple: "First, I wanted a unique number, but also 64 is the number my dad [Gene] wore [as a professional motorcycle racer] and my dad is the most special of all. He's the reason for any success I have."

Laurie Boschman

SOMETIMES SWEATER NUMBERS are just fun, and a pattern emerges out of nothing. Laurie Boschman was drafted by the Toronto Maple Leafs 9th overall in 1979 and he made the big team out of training camp that fall. He wanted to wear 10, which he had used throughout junior, but John Anderson was already using that number with the Leafs. Boschman opted for 12. When he was traded to Edmonton three years later, he wanted to keep 12, but the number was taken, so he went up two more numbers to 14. A year and a half later he was on the road again, this time to Winnipeg, but 14 was taken so he took 16. At that point he "promised to retire when he got to 20," but that never happened. He was acquired by New Jersey prior to the 1990–91 season, and amazingly 16 was available. His last stop, Ottawa, also had 16 ready and waiting for him. Boschman retired in 1993, having worn 12, 14, and 16, all because 10 had been taken during his rookie season.

31

RAY BOURQUE ARRIVED at his first NHL training camp with the Boston Bruins in 1979 and was assigned 29. Throughout the 1979–80 preseason schedule, Bourque wore that number, but when he made the team out of camp and arrived in the Bruins dressing room for his first regular season game, the Bruins had switched his sweater number to 7. Seven had not been worn in Boston since the hugely popular Phil Esposito was traded to the New York Rangers some years before. A number of years later, the Bruins announced they were going to retire Esposito's 7. The plan was that the Bruins would take the number out of circulation after Bourque retired. The day of the ceremony, Boston coach Terry O'Reilly met with Bourque and suggested he switch to 77. Bourque liked the idea. Prior to the ceremony, only O'Reilly, Bourque, and the team's trainer, who stitched the new number onto the sweater, knew the surprise Bourque had in store for Esposito that night. At centre ice, during Esposito's retirement ceremony, Bourque removed his 7 sweater and handed it to a surprised Esposito before turning around to show him his new number to the cheers of the sold-out crowd at the Boston Garden.

DARREN BOYKO PLAYED exactly one NHL game with his hometown Winnipeg Jets during the 1988–89 season, but he played in Finland, with HIFK Helsinki, for 11 of his 12 years in Europe. Whenever he got the chance he wore 10, a number he had used ever since he was a kid, because he believed that two numbers on his back made him look bigger than having a single digit. In that lone game with the Jets, however, 10 was on the back of the great Dale Hawerchuk, so Boyko had to go with 15, given to him by the trainers.

PINT-SIZED DANIEL BRIERE might not be the biggest
player in today's NHL, but he is one of the more
skilled forwards in the game, as his play for Canada
at the World Championship in 2003 and 2004
showed. Briere grew up wearing 8, and in junior,
with Drummondville, he wore 14. When he made
Phoenix full-time to start the 1998–99 season, he
wanted 14, but that number was taken by Mike
Stapleton. Briere settled for 8. In March 2003, Briere
was traded to Buffalo, where 14 had been retired by
the Sabres in honour of Rene Robert of the famed
French Connection line. As a result, Briere combined
his two favourite numbers to create 48 and he's been
wearing it ever since, both in the NHL and internation-
ally for Team Canada.

A NATIVE OF MICHIGAN, Dan Bylsma played Junior B hockey in Ontario in the late 1980s, where he was recruited by Bowling Green State University. One of the reasons Bylsma accepted Bowling Green's petition was that his brother, Scott, had played there a few years earlier. The university promised Dan that he could wear Scott's 21—he had already been wearing 21 in Jr. B—if he came there to play. Dan accepted and thus continued what became a career-long relationship with that number. After graduation, he made his way up the minor pro ranks and at every stop—Greensboro, Moncton, Phoenix—he was able to wear 21. He made his NHL debut with Los Angeles in 1995–96, but 21 was taken by Tony Granato so Bylsma simply doubled it and wore 42. After five seasons with the Kings, Bylsma signed as a free agent with Anaheim in the summer of 2000 and continued to wear 21 through to his retirement in the summer of 2004.

Dan Bylsma

Guy Carbonneau

IF ANY PLAYER could be called the second coming of Bob Gainey—the great defensive forward who also contributed to his team's offense—it was Guy Carbonneau. Over the course of his 19 NHL seasons, Carbonneau won three Stanley Cups and as many Selke Trophies in recognition of his skills at both ends of the ice. Amazingly, he wore 21 for every game of his career except the first two games as a rookie, in 1980–81. Carbonneau spent the first 13 years of his NHL career in Montreal and, after a year in St. Louis, played his last five seasons in Dallas, where he helped the Stars win the Cup in 1999. He also became a fan favourite during his time in Texas, so much so that after his retirement in the summer of 2000 the Stars Booster Club petitioned the team to retire Carbonneau's 21 for the 2000–01 season. Bob Gainey, the team's GM and Carbonneau's longtime teammate in Montreal, understood the motives of the Booster Club: "He's had a great impact on everyone," Gainey said. "The fans saw how hard he worked. They appreciated it.... We'll have to wait for that emotion to die down, and then we'll see. For now, though, nobody will be wearing his number this season." Five years later, the number remains out of circulation.

WENDEL CLARK was the NHL's first overall draft choice in 1985 and made the Leafs straight out of camp that fall, an 18-year-old with a heart much bigger than his body. Clark was given 17 by the trainers, a number that had no importance to him prior to his making the NHL, but from then on it was his number of choice. Clark was a Maple Leafs forward three times during his career, and each time he wore 17. When he was traded to Quebec at the start of the 1994–95 season, the same sweater number was awaiting him at Le Colisée. When he moved on to the New York Islanders a year later, Clark wore 17, and again when he went to Tampa Bay in 1998–99. In fact, his 17 was so well respected in Toronto that two incoming players who usually wore 17 changed numbers rather than use Clark's: In 1995, Mike Ridley came over from Washington and switched to 7; and in 1997 Kris King arrived from Phoenix and switched to 12. The only time Clark didn't wear that number was in the latter part of that season, when he was traded to the Detroit Red Wings. Doug Brown was already wearing 17, so Clark simply reversed the numbers and went with 71. When Clark signed with Chicago for 1999–2000, the Blackhawks had 17 waiting for him.

Bobby Clarke

WHEN FEISTY, 20-year-old Bobby Clarke joined the Philadelphia Flyers in 1969 just a few months after being drafted, the team gave him the 16 for which he became famous. In fact, he is the first and only player to wear that number for the Broad Street Bullies. His was a career that spanned 15 years, two Stanley Cup championships, and one Hall of Fame induction. To cap it off, when he retired in 1983, his 16 was hoisted to the rafters of the Spectrum as a final tribute to the popular captain. As iconic as Clarke and 16 are in Flyers' lore, he did wear a different number, albeit for just one game. "On the road, one time, someone stole my sweater and the only extra one we had had 36 on it," he explained. So, for one game, captain Clarke had no "C" on the front of his sweater and no 16 on the back.

GEOFF COURTNALL was a skilled left winger who reached the 20-goal mark ten times during his 17-year NHL career. Though he proved his skills around the net by scoring 367 career goals, he had far less luck getting the sweater number he wanted. Courtnall always wanted to wear 7, but when he first played with the Boston Bruins during the 1983–84 season, the number belonged to team captain Ray Bourque. After wearing 32 for a while, Courtnall decided simply to double the 7 and wear 14. The Bruins shipped him to Edmonton during the 1987–88 season, but Paul Coffey, who wore 7, had just left the team that year, and out of respect Courtnall wore 15 that season. On his next stop in Washington, Courtnall encountered another difficulty because the organization retired 7 in honour of Yvon Labre. So, Courtnall selected 14 and kept the number at his next stops in St. Louis and Vancouver, by this time happy being identified with his second choice, 14.

AFTER BEING DRAFTED 7th overall by the Toronto Maple Leafs in 1983, speedy forward Russ Courtnall wore 16 and 26 in Toronto before settling on 9 for the rest of his six years with the team (1983–89). After his infamous trade to the Montreal Canadiens for the less-talented John Kordic, Courtnall could no longer wear 9 because the number had been retired in honour of Maurice Richard. So Courtnall flipped the digit upside down and wore 6. When he was sent to Minnesota prior to 1992–93 season, Courtnall settled for 26 and wore it when the team moved to Dallas. The only other time he got to wear 9 again was during his stay with the Vancouver Canucks (1994–97). Courtnall finished his career wearing the less desirable 21 with the New York Rangers (1996–97) and 19 with Los Angeles Kings (1997–99).

TEEN SENSATION SIDNEY CROSBY has yet to play an NHL game, but when he does he will likely wear his first choice, 87—the number he has worn during his junior years with the Rimouski Oceanic in the Quebec Major Junior Hockey League (QMJHL). The number represents his birth year and birth date (August 7). When he played for Canada at the 2004 and 2005 World Junior Championship, though, Crosby reverted to 9 because Hockey Canada has a policy that no player may wear a number higher than 40. Number 9 was Crosby's number from his midget days with Dartmouth AAA.

BORN IN

A

87

51

MARCEL DIONNE is a Hall of Famer. Although in junior he had worn the prestigious number 9—the traditional number for a team's best player—he was assigned 5 with the Red Wings and, not being particularly superstitious, made no objections. Dionne quickly developed into a superstar. When captain and longtime Wings forward Alex Delvecchio retired during the 1973–74 season, he believed Dionne would be the successor to the captain's "C" and urged him to switch to 12, the number worn by Detroit great Sid Abel during the team's Cup-winning years in the early 1950s. "It was an incredible tribute for me to wear Sid Abel's number," Dionne recalled. Sure enough, Dionne was named captain for 1974–75. After one year he became a free agent and signed with the Los Angeles Kings who encouraged him to wear 9. Dionne refused because Gene Carr wore the number, and it was considered sacrilege for a player to take another player's number. "You can't take a number away from a player! Number 16 was available, so I took 16 and stuck with it." Dionne became one of the greatest players in NHL history. Number 16 is now retired in Los Angeles in Dionne's honour.

Shane Doan

AS A KID, Shane Doan was a defenceman and wore 4 in honour of his idol, Bobby Orr. When he played midget he wore 28, and asked for that number when he arrived in Kamloops, British Columbia, to play for the Blazers in the junior league. Unfortunately, the recently graduated Scott Niedermayer had made 28 famous with the team. "The only number available was 19 and I have held that number ever since," Doan related. "It's the highest 'scoring number' in the NHL [i.e., not many great scorers have ever worn a number higher than 19] and many captains wear 19, including Joe Sakic, Steve Yzerman, Joe Thornton, and Markus Naslund." Doan has worn 19 in every NHL game he has played, starting in 1995–96 with Winnipeg and continuing in Phoenix when the team moved south. He also tries to wears 19 in international tournaments for Team Canada.

CHRIS DRURY WORE 18 at Boston College because his older brother, Ted, had worn the number as a kid growing up in Boston. But when Chris arrived in the NHL with the Colorado Avalanche in 1998, Adam Deadmarsh already had 18, so Drury went with 37, the number he had been assigned in training camp. When Deadmarsh was traded to Los Angeles, Drury switched to 18. Teammate Alex Tanguay also wanted 18, but Drury had more seniority and got first dibs on the number. Five years and one Stanley Cup later, Drury was traded to the Calgary Flames with Stephane Yelle in a blockbuster deal that saw Derek Morris, Jeff Shantz, and Dean McAmmond head to Colorado. In Calgary, Drury reverted to 37, a number that the outgoing McAmmond had worn. Later that season, the Avs traded McAmmond back to Calgary and Drury offered him 37 back, taking 18 as a replacement.

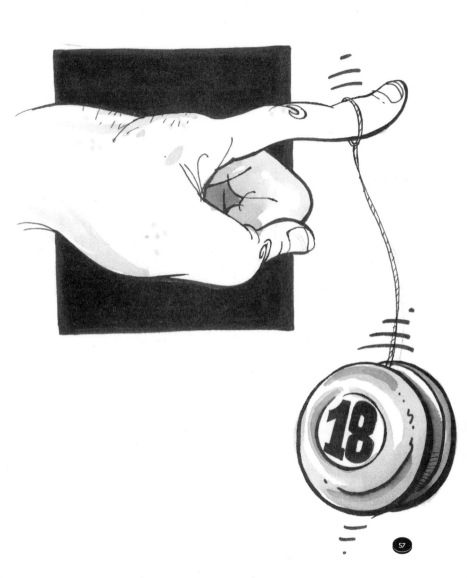

Ron Ellis

RON ELLIS PLAYED ONE GAME for the Toronto Maple Leafs as a call-up at the end of the 1963–64 season before rejoining his junior team, the Toronto Marlies, for the playoffs and winning the Memorial Cup. That fall he made the big club, and coach Punch Imlach awarded the rookie the prestigious 11 sweater, the number the coach reserved for his favourite newcomer. Imlach was perhaps the most superstitious coach in league history. Ellis scored 23 goals that season, finishing runner-up to goalie Roger Crozier of Detroit for the Calder Trophy. The next year Imlach reassigned the 11 to favourite rookie Brit Selby, who won the Calder that season. Ellis reverted to the 8 worn during his Marlies career, but a couple of years later he was given special dispensation by Ace Bailey to wear 6. That number had been retired since 1933 after Bailey's career ended as a result of a vicious Eddie Shore check. Ellis and Bailey became friends and Ace permitted the team's young star the honour of wearing 6. Ellis retired in 1975, and so did the number, but when he returned to the team two years later, he again adopted 6. Ellis retired for good during the 1980–81 season and that number has not been worn since.

TORONTO

FOR RON!

RUSSIAN-BORN SERGEI FEDOROV defected from the CCCP national team while in Portland, Oregon, just before the start of the 1990 Goodwill Games. He had been drafted by the Detroit Red Wings while living in the Soviet Union the previous year. When he arrived at the Joe Louis Arena, Fedorov was so in awe of his idol, captain Steve Yzerman, that he copied everything the future Hall of Famer did, right down to wearing the same equipment. He couldn't wear Yzerman's 19 sweater, so he did the next best thing: he inverted the numbers and wore 91, the only number he has ever worn in the NHL.

Sergei Fedorov

Theo Fleury

TROUBLED, PINT-SIZED superstar Theo Fleury became famous in Calgary while wearing 14, but he holds the distinction of being one of two players in NHL history to wear two numbers in the same game (the other was Martin Rucinsky). On the night of December 7, 1998, a bad cut bloodied Fleury's sweater. Referee Marc Faucette told him he had to change jerseys before he could return to the ice. There was no other 14 sweater in the dressing room, so Fleury took one from a fan behind the Flames' bench. Faucette, however, ruled that the many autographs on that souvenir sweater made it unwearable for game conditions. Fleury went to the dressing room, returned with a 74, and finished the game with that number. Fleury usually wears 74 in international play, as he did during the Salt Lake Olympics, because the more senior Brendan Shanahan claimed 14. Fleury didn't mind because the stylized "7" and "1" looked so close he felt as if he had on 14 anyway. Fleury liked 74 so much that when he made his return to hockey in January 2005 with the Horse Lake Thunder in the North Peace Hockey League, a senior hockey team in Alberta, he wore that number rather than the 14 for which he is more famous.

COLORADO AVALANCHE defenceman Adam Foote was assigned 52 during his first training camp with the Quebec Nordiques in 1991. The number felt comfortable almost immediately to the 20-year-old. Foote had worn 5 during his junior career with the Sault Ste. Marie Greyhounds, and wore 2 in pee-wee, so the combination of these numbers felt like a good omen. After a solid first season in the NHL, Foote decided to keep the unusual number and wore 52 even when he played for Team Canada at the Olympic Games in 1998 and 2002.

HALL OF FAMER Mike Gartner played 1,432 regular season games in the NHL before retiring in 1998. During his 19 seasons and five-team tour of duty he wore only two numbers, 11 and 22. He wore 9 with the Niagara Falls junior team, but this was the traditional number for star players in the NHL, so when he joined the Washington Capitals in 1979 he took 11 because of his admiration for Gilbert Perreault. Gartner stayed with the Caps for a decade, and when he was traded to the Minnesota North Stars 11 was waiting for him. On March 6, 1990, he was sent to the Rangers, but 11 was taken so he doubled the number and took 22. When he moved on to the Leafs four years later, he was able to wear 11, but his final stop, in Phoenix, required a return to 22.

NEW YORK ISLANDERS forward Clark Gillies was an inspiration to his teammates throughout his career. He spent the first 12 years of his career with the Isles (1974–86), winning four Stanley Cups and scoring more than 30 goals six times. He wore 9 in honour of his idol, Bobby Hull, one of the most famous players to wear that number. When Gilles was claimed on waivers by Buffalo, however, he ran into difficulty because Scott Arniel was the incumbent 9. For the 1986–87 season, Gillies wore 39, and the following year opted for the simpler 90, which incorporated his cherished number for his final NHL season.

THESE DAYS, Doug Gilmour and 93 are synonymous, but the fact is that he didn't adopt the number until halfway through his ninth NHL season. Gilmour wore 18 and 9 with the St. Louis Blues at the start of his career. When he was traded to the Calgary Flames, Lanny McDonald, the team's beloved captain, wore 9. Gilmour took 39 with the Flames, but when he was traded to the Toronto Maple Leafs, he adopted the more unusual number, 93. Gilmour was urged by the team's executives to wear a more traditional number, such as 14 or 16. The Maple Leafs marketing department especially loved the idea of their new star wearing 14, a number made famous in Toronto by another great centre, Dave Keon. Gilmour had different ideas and kept 93, the number he had worn while playing softball with the Flames during the summer. While Gilmour was the first Flame to wear 39 on ice, the digits were not available on the ball team, so he inverted them and grew to like the 93. Gilmour kept number 93 in subsequent stints with the New Jersey Devils, Chicago Blackhawks, Buffalo Sabres, Montreal Canadiens, and his one-game return to Toronto at the end of his career in 2002–03.

WHILE THE TREND of "doubling up" single digits helped solve the occasional number quandary, players whose number of choice already contains two digits need to find another option when their preferred number is unavailable. Many choose to simply invert their number. One of the first players to do this was Butch Goring. When he joined the New York Islanders from Los Angeles at the trade deadline of the 1979–80 season, he couldn't wear his familiar 19 because it belonged to Bryan Trottier. Goring took 21 for the balance of the year and the Islanders went on to win their first Stanley Cup. The following season, he hit the ice with 91—the inverse of his preferred 19—and his luck continued. The Islanders won three more Stanley Cups in the succeeding three years.

John Grahame

WHEN HE WAS about 13 years old playing goal in his hometown of Denver, Colorado, John Grahame was invited to represent his state at a special camp for the 50 best young goalies in the United States (one from every state). When he got there he was assigned a 47 to stick on his sweater (much like racers at a track meet peel and stick numbers on their chest). Ever since then, Grahame has been 47, and wherever he goes there is little chance of conflict with another player already wearing the odd number. He began his NHL career wearing the number with Boston (1999–2003) and continued to do so when he was traded to the Tampa Bay Lightning in January 2003.

COLORADO AVALANCHE forward Chris Gratton has always worn 77 when it's been available during his NHL career. He favours the number because of family ties. "I wore it in junior," he began. "My cousin wore that number when he played for the Oshawa Generals. I always told myself if I ever got to play in the OHL I'd wear 77 as well." Gratton was a first-round draft choice of the Tampa Bay Lightning in 1993 and wore 77 with the team that fall. In May 1997, Gratton joined the Philadelphia Flyers, and he had to find a new number because legendary defenceman Paul Coffey was wearing 77. Gratton ruled out 66 because that was Mario Lemieux's number and there was no chance he was going to wear 99. Gratton's fondness for "doubled up" numbers resulted in his selecting 55. During the 1998–99 season, Gratton was traded back to Tampa Bay. At the time, the team was on the road and didn't have a 77 sweater on hand so Gratton wore 20. Gratton kept 77 in Buffalo and Phoenix, but a trade to Colorado late in the 2003–04 season meant he had to choose a new number because the Avalanche retired 77 to honour Ray Bourque. Gratton settled for 24.

WAYNE GRETZKY'S FAMOUS 99, like Phil Esposito's 77 in the 1970s, was the result of a player looking for another number when the first choice was unavailable. Gretzky grew up idolizing Gordie Howe, who wore 9, and as a kid Gretzky wore that number whenever he could. But when Gretzky arrived in the Ontario Hockey League (OHL) to play junior hockey in Sault Ste. Marie in 1977, 9 was on the back of veteran forward Brian Gualazzi. Gretzky tried 19 and 25, but these didn't feel right to him. The team's coach, Muzz MacPherson, suggested that perhaps Gretzky should simply wear two 9s. Gretzky agreed, and the next game he skated on the ice with 99 stitched on the back of his Soo Greyhounds sweater, ushering in the most famous sweater number in hockey history. When Gretzky retired from the NHL in 1999, his 99 was retired league-wide, the first and only number so honoured.

FORWARD JEFF HALPERN was born in Potomac, Maryland, and grew up a fan of the Washington Capitals, the team he would ultimately sign with in 1999 after four seasons of NCAA hockey. One of the first "stars" of the longtime hapless Capitals' franchise was future Hall of Fame forward Mike Gartner. When Halpern made his NHL debut in 1999 with the team, ten years after Gartner left Washington, he chose 11, in part because Gartner was his childhood idol and also because that was the number his father wore when Halpern Sr. played sports.

STEVE HEINZE PLAYED nine seasons with the Boston Bruins wearing 23 (1991–2000) a common number, but not his first choice. He wanted to wear 57 in playful reference to the steak sauce, but the management of a staid, Original Six team was not about to have him treat the gold and black of Boston irreverently. When Heinze joined the expansion Columbus Blue Jackets for the 2000–01 season, the team was only too happy to spiff his sweater up with a 57. When he was sent to the Buffalo Sabres late in that same season, Heinze kept the playful number. In the off-season, he signed with Los Angeles where he played the final two years of his career (2001–03), keeping the "saucy" 57 on his back. Similarly, Shawn Heins wore 57 with Pittsburgh during the 2002–03 season.

SOME MODERN-DAY goaltenders choose unusual numbers simply to avoid such mundane and traditional numbers as 1, 30, and 31. Ron Hextall wanted to wear 30 when he came up with the Philadelphia Flyers as a rookie in 1986, but the number already belonged to another young netminder, Darren Jensen. The team offered Hextall the choice of 27 (previously worn by goaltender Gilles Meloche with California, Cleveland, Minnesota, and Pittsburgh) or the equally rare 33. Hextall liked 27 and went on to lead the Flyers to the Stanley Cup finals. He won the Conn Smythe trophy, and was named the league's rookie of the year. When he was dealt to the New York Islanders in the summer of 1993, he found that Derek King had been wearing 27 for several seasons. Hextall chose to invert his favourite digits to create 72, making him the only NHL goaltender ever to wear that number.

Ken Hodge

KEN HODGE WORE 14 when he joined the NHL in 1964–65 with the Chicago Blackhawks, but when he was sent to Boston with Phil Esposito in one of the biggest trades in league history, he switched to 8. Hodge became a superstar in Beantown, won two Stanley Cups, and played with the team for 11 years. But in the summer of 1976, he was traded to the New York Rangers for Rick Middleton, creating a problem for Hodge because Steve Vickers was already wearing 8 with the Blueshirts. Hodge made history when he simply added another 8 to his number to make 88, thus becoming the first player to double up on a single digit to ensure that his favourite number stayed on his back.

Gordie Howe

HE WAS THE GREATEST 9 of them all, but Gordie Howe, like so many Hall of Famers, started his career with an all-too-obscure number. In his case, that number was 17, which Howe wore with the Detroit Red Wings in 1946–47 as an 18-year-old rookie. Before the start of the next season, Roy Conacher, who wore 9 during Howe's rookie season, was sold to Chicago. Red Wings trainer Lefty Wilson told Howe to take the number, but Howe demurred, saying he was quite happy with 17, thank you. The wily trainer pointed out that a low number meant a lower and more comfortable berth on trains. In a blink of an eye, Howe switched to 9 and travelled comfortably on road trips the rest of his career.

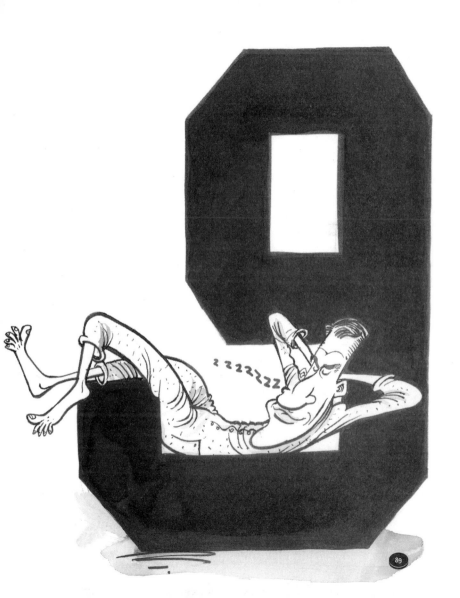

Cristobal Huet

GOALTENDER CRISTOBAL HUET (pronounced "Hewitt") always wanted to wear 39 because he was born on September 3—the third day of the ninth month. But when the NHL's first goalie born in France got to Los Angeles in 2002, he was given 35 and decided to keep the number for good luck. Huet tries to wear 39 in international tournaments and the French national team has been able to accommodate him so far, most recently at the 2004 World Championship and the final 2005 Olympic qualification tournament.

AT THE END OF his third outstanding season with the Kamloops Blazers of the Western Hockey League (WHL), junior sensation Jarome Iginla was called up to the Calgary Flames for two playoff games in the spring of 1996. He had been given 12 his first year with the Blazers, but when he got to the Saddledome he found that Paul Kruse had that number. Iginla settled for 24 instead. Midway through the following season, Iginla, now an established player with Calgary, came into his lucky number when Kruse was traded to the Islanders. He immediately took 12, a number he has worn ever since, and he has gone on to become one of the finest all-around players in the world.

WHEN JAROMIR JAGR made his North American debut with the Pittsburgh Penguins in 1990, he sported 68, the first NHL player to wear that number. It signified the year that Soviet tanks rolled through Wenceslas Square in Prague to crush the Czech uprising and provided Jagr with a constant reminder of his heritage. At every level and every game since 1990, he has worn 68. During the NHL lockout of 2004–05, Jagr signed with Kladno in the Czech Republic's Extraleague. After a short stint, he left to play for Avangard Omsk in the Russian league at a much higher salary and, ironically, wore 68 with that team. So, while playing on Russian ice, and being paid by a Russian team, Jagr wore a number that was intended to protest that country's previous regime against his own Czech Republic.

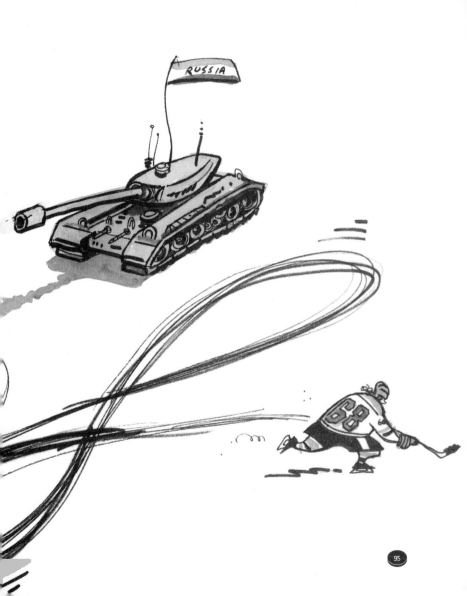

JOE JUNEAU WAS DRAFTED in 1988 at the end of his first season with RPI. He remained in college and got his degree before playing for Team Canada in 1991–92, including the Albertville Olympics. After that, he joined the Boston Bruins and there encountered a numeric problem. In Albertville, as with every other place he had played previously, Juneau wore 9, but when he got to the Bruins, that number had been placed high in the rafters of the Garden in honour of Johnny Bucyk. The 24-year-old Juneau had the temerity to ask Bucyk if he could wear the number, and Bucyk agreed—so long as Juneau gave Bucyk the six-figure signing bonus Juneau had just received. Juneau declined and instead wore 49 during his three years with the Bruins; the "4" representing Bobby Orr, the "9" standing for his favourite number. At almost every stop during his six-team NHL career, Juneau had a 9 on his sweater, always choosing 90 except 1999–2000 in Ottawa where he went with 39 after starting with 28 for a short time.

Dave Keon

FROM A SWEATER NUMBER perspective, Dave Keon was one of the rarest of players in that he wore the same number in every NHL game he played. In junior, he wore 9 with the St. Mike's Majors in Toronto, but when he joined the Toronto Maple Leafs in 1960, Dick Duff was wearing the number. Keon was given 14 by the team's trainers simply because it was available (Rudy Migay wore the number the previous year, but he got hurt and retired; Ted Hampson also wore 14 that year, but he wasn't a full-time player). Keon went on to wear 14 for every NHL game he played: some 1,388 combined regular season and playoff games with the Leafs and the Hartford Whalers over 18 seasons!

TORONTO
MAPLE
LEAFS

C

14

×18
=1388?

IN 1985, AS A YOUNG rookie with the Detroit Red Wings, Petr Klima scored 32 goals wearing the unusual 85 on his back. Though Klima's goal scoring was impressive, even more interesting was how he came to pursue his dream of playing in the NHL. Klima was drafted in 1983 by Detroit while living in the former Czechoslovakia, but to join the Wings he had to defect from his homeland. The 85 represented the year that Klima left Czechoslovakia and came to North America. Because it was such an unusual number, he was able to wear it throughout his career: five years with the Red Wings (1985–90), four years with Edmonton (1989–93), three years with Tampa Bay (1993–96), partial seasons with Los Angeles, Pittsburgh, and Edmonton again (1996–97), and a final season back in Detroit (1998–99).

A SUPERB SKATER and natural goalscorer, Ilya Kovalchuk always wore 17 in tribute to his hero, Valeri Kharlamov. "I don't want to look like him and I don't want to play like him," he explained. "I just like him as a player." Kharlamov died before Kovalchuk was born (in 1983), but the young Russian star learned of the great Soviet forward from his own father, who regaled young Ilya with stories of Kharlamov's greatness. Kovalchuk joined the Atlanta Thrashers in the fall of 2001 and has worn 17 for his whole NHL career to date. In international tournaments he reverses the digits and plays with 71, most notably in the 2004 World Cup of Hockey and 2005 World Championship.

Ilya Kovalchuk

WHEN ANDREI KOVALENKO arrived with the Quebec Nordiques in 1992, he wanted 26, the number he had worn with CSKA in the Soviet league. However, 26 had been used by the great Peter Stastny and the team wouldn't give that number to the newcomer. Kovalenko recalled his days living in the First District in Balakovo, Soviet Union, when he attended School 5. Thus, he decided to wear 51 and got the latter with the Quebec Nordiques. Amazingly, in his ten years in the NHL, he wore 51 with six teams—Quebec, Colorado, Montreal, Edmonton, Carolina, and Boston. The only time he didn't get 51 was during his brief stay with the Philadelphia Flyers (1998–99), where he wore 25 and 15.

GUY LAFLEUR ARRIVED in Montreal in the fall of 1971 after being drafted first overall by the Canadiens. During his spectacular junior career with the Quebec Remparts, where he led the team to the coveted Memorial Cup during his final season, Lafleur always wore 4. When he got to the Forum, the team wanted him to continue to wear 4, not only to please him but also to signal the arrival of the new Jean Beliveau, the most recent and famous wearer of that number with les Canadiens. Beliveau was willing to bring the number out of retirement, but Lafleur refused. "I have great respect for Jean Beliveau and always admired him as a man and player," he said at the time. Instead, he opted for 10, in large part because the last man to wear that number for any length of time was little-known Ted Harris. Wearing 10 would give no pressure to the 20-year-old Lafleur. "The Flower" went on to have a Hall of Fame career and retired in 1984 as one of the greatest Canadiens of all time. When he mounted a comeback in 1988, he returned to the NHL wearing his well-known 10, first for the New York Rangers and later the Quebec Nordiques.

GUY LAPOINTE WORE 5 for his whole career, first in Montreal, then in St. Louis, but it was during his last tour of duty, in Boston, that a kerfuffle about his number arose. The Bruins signed him for the 1983–84 season, but Dit Clapper's 5 was retired in 1947 and had not been used since. The Bruins wanted Bobby Orr to wear 5 when he entered the league in 1966, but Clapper objected and Orr refused to insult the great Dit. By the time Lapointe arrived, Clapper was dead and unable to voice his opposition to unretiring 5. When Dit's relatives saw Lapointe in their father's number, they were outraged but powerless. Many fans sided with the family, and while the team made Lapointe happy and ensured he wore the same number his whole career, it upset many who cherished the team's history and one of its Hall of Fame players.

Georges Laraque

IT'S NOT UNUSUAL to hear of a scorer who idolizes a scorer, or a defenceman who wants to be like Bobby Orr. But Edmonton Oilers tough guy Georges Laraque's idol was New York Islanders sniper Mike Bossy, a completely different player from Laraque, who made his way through the ranks mostly with his fists. During his younger days and junior career in the Quebec Major Junior Hockey League (QMJHL), Laraque always wore 22 in tribute to Bossy. But when Laraque got to the NHL, the number wasn't available in Edmonton. He chose 27, a number he's worn faithfully since entering the league in 1997–98.

PIERRE LAROUCHE was a skilled centre who spent 14 seasons frustrating NHL goaltenders with four different clubs. He was a highly touted offensive talent when the Pittsburgh Penguins made him the 8th overall selection in the 1974 Amateur Draft. He joined the Penguins and selected sweater 10. During his fourth season in Pittsburgh, he was traded to the Montreal Canadiens, where the presence of the legendary Guy Lafleur made wearing that number impossible. Larouche arrived at a creative solution by deciding to wear 28. Simple arithmetic illustrates that 2 plus 8 equals 10, so Larouche

was able to keep his link to his preferred number. After a short stop in Hartford, Larouche joined his fourth and final NHL club when he signed with the New York Rangers in 1983. On Broadway, his number story came full circle. Larouche, who wore his old 10 with the Rangers, must have had a sense of déjà vu during the training camp of 1988 because that year Lafleur decided to end his three-season retirement and join the Broadway Blueshirts. When Lafleur arrived in New York, he found Larouche wearing his 10 and instead took 44. However, Larouche retired before the 1988–89 season began and Lafleur immediately adopted his 10 sweater.

IN 1983, BRIAN LAWTON became the first American selected first overall in the NHL draft, so he was saddled with great expectations when he joined the North Stars in hockey-mad Minnesota that fall. The expectations were heightened when Lawton stepped on the ice for his NHL debut wearing 98, just one digit lower than the 99 worn by the legendary Wayne Gretzky, who at that time was at the peak of his powers. The reality of the situation was that as an 18-year-old expected to be the saviour for a moribund franchise, Lawton didn't need the additional pressure of wearing a number that drew comparisons to Gretzky. He soon dropped the 9 and simply wore 8. He then switched to 11 the following season, but the new numbers couldn't change his luck, as Lawton never came close to playing like the Great One. Lawton bounced to five other NHL clubs before retiring in 1993.

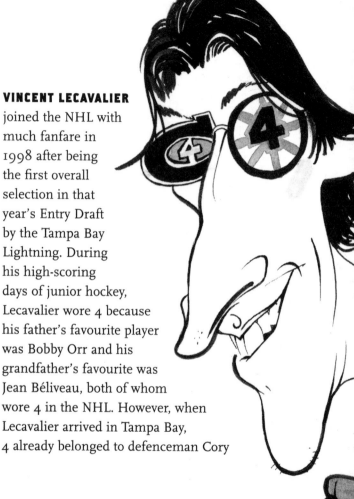

VINCENT LECAVALIER

VINCENT LECAVALIER joined the NHL with much fanfare in 1998 after being the first overall selection in that year's Entry Draft by the Tampa Bay Lightning. During his high-scoring days of junior hockey, Lecavalier wore 4 because his father's favourite player was Bobby Orr and his grandfather's favourite was Jean Béliveau, both of whom wore 4 in the NHL. However, when Lecavalier arrived in Tampa Bay, 4 already belonged to defenceman Cory

Cross, so the young superstar added two fours together and wore 8. But Lecavalier had to wait only one season before opportunity knocked and he was allowed to wear his preferred 4. Early in the 1999–2000 season, the Lightning made a trade with the Toronto Maple Leafs that sent Cory Cross north and freed up 4 for Lecavalier, who wasted no time in heading to the dressing room to make the switch from 8 to 4.

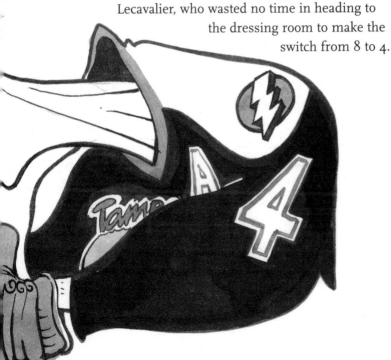

GRANT LEDYARD PATROLLED the NHL bluelines for 18 seasons (1984–2002) with nine different NHL clubs and wore several different numbers. He established himself as a regular NHL defenceman with his fourth club, the Buffalo Sabres, where he settled on 3 as his sweater number. However, he didn't stick with that number for long. When he joined the Dallas Stars in 1993, Ledyard switched to a new number. Unfortunately, the change was spurred on by a personal tragedy. Ledyard's father, Hal, was a quarterback in the Canadian Football League with the Winnipeg Blue Bombers and the Saskatchewan Roughriders in the 1960s and wore 12 during his career. When Hal drowned off the coast of San Diego, the younger Ledyard opted to switch to his father's number. For the rest of his career, whenever he could, Grant Ledyard took 12 in tribute.

IT IS NOT MERELY COINCIDENCE that Mario Lemieux's trademark number is the upside-down image of Wayne Gretzky's equally iconic 99. Even as a youngster, Mario Lemieux's talent was so undeniable that he was already being represented by the same agents who worked for Gretzky. During those years, Lemieux would often wear 12 or 27, the same digits his older brother, Alain, wore when playing hockey. However, when Mario was about to start his junior career with the Laval Titans, he made a change. Lemieux's agents, Bob Perno and Gus Badali, urged Mario to pick out a more distinct sweater number. Lemieux had figured he would continue to wear 27, but Perno pointed out that he and Alain had separate careers, and as such, their numbers should be different. "Mario, I think you're going to be one of the best players of all time," he said. "To me, the best player of all time is Wayne Gretzky." Confused, Lemieux asked if he wanted him to wear 99. Perno continued, "There's only one Wayne Gretzky, and only one Mario Lemieux," Perno explained. "Why not 66? It's 99 upside down. People will compare you to Gretzky, but won't criticize you." That fall, Lemieux took to the ice with the Laval Titans wearing 66 on his back and a legend was born.

Brett Lindros

THE YOUNGER, BIGGER brother of Eric began his junior career with the Kingston Frontenacs in 1992 in the shadow of Eric, who had been a dominant force in the Ontario Hockey League (OHL) as a member of the Oshawa Generals. Much like his brother, who has a "trademark" number with his 88, Brett started his career with the equally unique 75. He didn't choose the number just because it is rare, though that was certainly part of it. It was the year of Brett's birth. When he made the leap to the NHL with the New York Islanders, as their first-round draft pick in 1994, he did so wearing 75. However, the number didn't seem quite as unique with high-profile teammates wearing 68 (Ziggy Palffy) and 72 (Mathieu Schneider). Unfortunately, Lindros was unable to make a name for himself or his number on Long Island. In just his second season, with only 51 NHL games to his credit, he suffered a career-ending concussion and was forced to retire.

Eric Lindros

THE "BIG E" exploded onto the hockey scene in the early 1990s as an unstoppable force whose physical prowess and soft hands made him a dominant force in the Ontario Hockey League (OHL) and got him anointed as the "next one" in the NHL. Lindros arrived in the NHL in 1992 surrounded by controversy when he snubbed the team that drafted him, the Quebec Nordiques, and forced a trade that landed him with the Philadelphia Flyers. When he made his NHL debut in the fall of 1992, he did so already having a unique number on his back. Many fans assumed that Lindros' 88 was a conscious choice to wear a number that would be similar to Wayne Gretzky's 99 and Mario Lemieux's 66 as an iconic double-digit sweater number, but that was not the case. Lindros, in his younger days, always wore 8 to honour his friend and mentor, the late John McCauley, who wore the number as an NHL referee. However, when Lindros' junior career began in 1989 with the Oshawa Generals, 8 was not available. So, much like Gretzky did years before, Lindros doubled up the digit and wore 88. By the time he was an NHL rookie with the Flyers, the number had become part of his identity.

IN 1979, KEVIN LOWE was the first ever NHL draft pick of the Edmonton Oilers. The defenceman went on to win five Stanley Cups with the club during his illustrious career. Lowe's older cousin, Mike Lowe, wore 6 so Kevin decided that would be his number as well. Mike was such a skilled player that he was drafted by the St. Louis Blues 19th overall in 1969. Lowe admired him and stuck with the number no matter what. When he began his junior career with the Quebec Remparts, the team gave him 6, but when he arrived in Edmonton, they gave him 4. "I never said anything. Who would?" Even if he had objected to 4, it wouldn't have done him any good because Colin Campbell was wearing 6. Campbell, with five years of NHL experience, clearly had the seniority and the claim to the number, but "Later that year, Colin Campbell told me I could buy it [the number] from him. I passed on his offer." Lowe spent 15 seasons on the Oilers' blueline, and the 4 treated him well. He not only captained the club, but also joined the front office upon his retirement. Though the number is not officially retired in Edmonton, no other player has worn 4 since Lowe hung up his skates.

WINGER ERIC MELOCHE is the son of former NHL goaltender Gilles Meloche, whose most notable years came with the Minnesota North Stars. Meloche senior wore 27 during much of his career—a unique selection for a netminder. When Eric began his career, he decided to wear a number that would pay tribute to his father but still be a unique number, so he reversed the digits and wore 72. Eric and his father's career intersected during the 2001–02 season when Eric made his NHL debut, wearing 72 with the Pittsburgh Penguins. Gilles Meloche ended his 18-year career in 1988 with the very same team.

ALEXANDER MOGILNY had recorded two seasons with more than 30 goals when he started the 1992–93 campaign with the Buffalo Sabres, but nobody could have predicted the scoring outburst that he had in store. Mogilny, who was paired on a line with the gifted Pat LaFontaine that year, terrorized NHL goaltenders and racked up 76 goals in 77 games. Mogilny was selected in 1988 and made history when he became the first Soviet player to defect and join an NHL club. In 1989, the World Championship was held in Sweden. The Soviet Union team, which included Mogilny, captured gold in that tournament, but immediately after the victory its young sniper secretly boarded a plan and flew to Buffalo. That fall, when Mogilny arrived in the Sabres' dressing room, he was surprised to see a sweater with his name and 89 stitched on the back of it. The unusual sweater number represented the year of his defection, but Mogilny had another coincidental link to the number. "I was the 89th pick in the draft and I came to North America in 1989," Mogilny recalls. "Wearing 89 on my back is special to me. It's more than just a number." In subsequent stops in Vancouver, New Jersey, and Toronto, Mogilny has continued to wear 89.

DEFECTED 1989

DRAFTED 89

131

THE GREAT HOWIE MORENZ delighted fans with his high-scoring ways as a member of the Montreal Canadiens in the 1920s. By the time his career ended with his tragic death, his 7 was famous in hockey circles but the humble beginnings of 7 on Morenz's back were quite trivial. Morenz signed his contract with the Canadiens on the 7th of July, 1923, and, as a result, manager Leo Dandurand assigned him 7. It wasn't just the date that gave the number significance to Dandurand; it also represented his own birthdate, so he felt those two facts combined made the number suitable for his new acquisition. After 11 seasons starring with the Canadiens, Morenz was traded to the Chicago Blackhawks in 1934. Years later, Dandurand commented, "When I gave a dinner for Morenz just prior to his leaving the Canadiens to play for the Chicago Blackhawks in the autumn of 1934, I told the guests that as long as I was associated with the Canadiens, no other player would wear number 7." His words proved true. The only other time a Habs player wore 7 after that day was in 1936 when Morenz himself was re-acquired by the Canadiens.

MARK NAPIER WORE the prestigious 9 when he started his professional hockey career in 1975 with the World Hockey Association's (WHA) Toronto Toros. Napier made the leap to the NHL for the 1978–79 season. He was assigned 31, a number usually reserved for goaltenders. In 1985, Napier landed in Edmonton, where he took sweater 18 (doubling his former 9, which belonged to Glenn Anderson). The acquisition of veteran Danny Gare by the Oilers spurred a number change for Napier. Gare had always worn 18 during his career, and Napier gave up 18 to Gare and switched to the unusual 65. Napier adopted the new digits for good reason. Napier had become the honourary chairman of the Cystic Fibrosis Foundation. The term "cystic fibrosis" is difficult for children to pronounce, and after one young patient referred to the disease as "sixty-five roses," that name was coined for the foundation. Every time someone inquired about his unusual number, Napier called attention to the foundation. A few years later, veteran tough guy Tim Hunter joined the Quebec Nordiques in 1992, and also wore 65. Like Napier, Hunter was the chairman of the Cystic Fibrosis Foundation during his time in Calgary.

SIXTY FIVE ROSES!

IT TOOK RIC NATTRESS 11 years to finally get the sweater number of his choice. Growing up playing hockey, Nattress had always worn 5. When he arrived in the NHL with Montreal in 1982, the number was the property of the Habs' new acquisition, Rick Green. Nattress, who felt that defencemen should wear a low number, looked for something else. Number 4 wasn't an option for him for two reasons: one, it had been retired in Montreal in honour of Jean Beliveau; two, Nattress had so much respect for the legendary Bobby Orr that he refused to wear that number (as a child, Nattress had attended Orr's hockey camp). Nattress settled on 3. Just before the 1985–86 season, the Canadiens traded the defenceman to the St. Louis Blues where he was given 27, which he wore until his trade to the Calgary Flames two years later. In Calgary, Nattress' 5 was taken by Neil Sheehy, so he went for 6. Nattress' next trade sent him to Toronto, where 5 has been out of circulation since 1951 as a tribute to the late Bill Barilko. Nattress selected 2, his fourth sweater number with as many teams. At the end of that season, Nattress signed with the Philadelphia Flyers for the 1992–93 season. He was finally able to wear 5 for his final year in the NHL.

PETR NEDVED WAS SELECTED 2nd overall in the 1990 Entry Draft, making him the highest drafted Czech player to that date. He made the leap to the NHL that same fall and wore 19 with the Vancouver Canucks. After three seasons with the Canucks, Nedved could not come to come to terms on a new contract with Vancouver. While the contract dispute spilled into the start of the 1993–94 season, Nedved obtained Canadian citizenship. Awaiting a trade to a new NHL team, he joined the Canadian National Team in time to play in the 1994 Olympic Winter Games in Lillehammer, Norway. Nedved officially became a Canadian citizen in 1993, so he took to the ice in Norway for Team Canada with 93 on his back. Shortly after the Olympics, Nedved returned to the NHL with the St. Louis Blues and continued to wear 93. He wore the number during his stints with the Rangers and Penguins, but it wasn't until a trade to the Edmonton Oilers late in the 2003–04 season that he got to honour his Canadian citizenship while playing for a team based in his adopted country.

FEISTY FINNISH WINGER Ville Nieminen made a name for himself in the 2004 Stanley Cup playoffs with his inspired, gritty play with the Calgary Flames. Twenty years earlier in the NHL playoffs, another feisty Finnish winger turned heads in Alberta and went on to have a great career as a top penalty killer and "super pest." That player was Esa Tikkanen, and Nieminen grew up a huge fan of his countryman. When Nieminen started his career in Finland, he wore 10 as a tribute to his boyhood idol. When he first cracked the NHL with the Colorado Avalanche in 1999, he was assigned 39 as a rookie, but switched to 10 for his second season. When he moved on to Pittsburgh, Nieminen continued to honour Tikkanen by wearing 10, but he had to switch to 20 in Chicago and 24 in Calgary because both teams already had 10 in circulation. Dave Lowry has since left the Flames, so fans in Alberta can expect Nieminen to switch to 10 the first chance he gets.

Ville Nieminen

ALTHOUGH OWEN NOLAN was the first overall pick in the 1990 NHL Entry Draft, he wasn't surrounded by the usual hype that accompanies a top prospect, mainly because the player touted to go first overall the *following* season was garnering all the attention. That player was Eric Lindros, and when Nolan arrived at his first NHL training camp he decided to take a playful swipe at his Ontario Hockey League (OHL) nemesis, who was still a junior player with the Oshawa Generals. Lindros' 88 was already well known, so Nolan decided to "demystify" the number and make his NHL debut in 1990 with the Quebec Nordiques wearing 88. Nolan's rookie season was a struggle as he and the team enjoyed very little success. Along the way, Nolan decided to drop the unfamiliar 88 and wear 11, his digits from his successful junior hockey days in Cornwall. The switch seemed to help, as Nolan eventually developed into one of the league's premier power forwards.

ALEXANDER OVECHKIN HAS yet to play in the NHL, but the first overall draft choice by Washington in 2004 knows he'll wear 8 when he gets the chance. That was the number his mother Tatiana wore while playing on two Olympic gold-medal basketball teams for the Soviet Union in 1976 and 1980. Ovechkin, a highly skilled forward who is the foundation for the rebuilding of the Capitals, comes from a great sports lineage. Not only is his mother a two-time gold medalist, but also his father was a great athlete in his own right, playing professional soccer in the former Soviet Union. If Ovechkin can get his coveted 8 in Washington, which currently belongs to defenceman Steve Eminger, it will be fitting tribute to a mother in a family of top-level athletes.

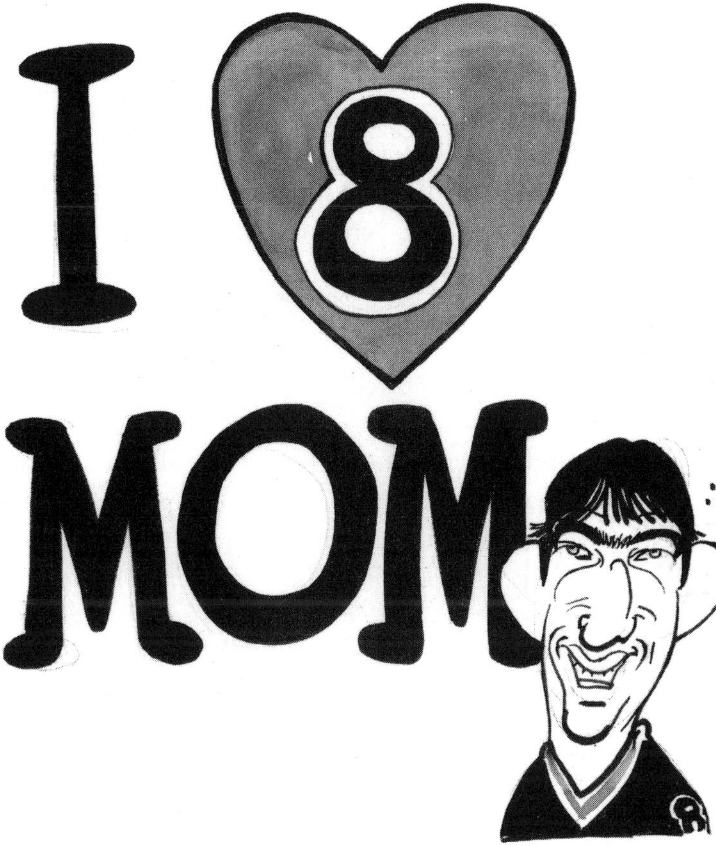
I
8
MOM

GILBERT PERREAULT WAS the heart and soul of the Buffalo Sabres from their birth as an expansion team in 1970 until his retirement in 1987. He was the first great star of the Sabres, centring their famous French Connection line. Perreault wore the number 11 for two reasons. First, his coach in his rookie season with the Sabres was Punch Imlach. Imlach, who was a superstitious type, was well known for giving his top rookie 11, which he considered his luckiest number. Second, at the 1970 Amateur Draft, the two expansion franchises, Vancouver and Buffalo, spun a wheel to determine who would select first overall. NHL president Clarence Campbell asked the Canucks to select "even" or "odd" for the spin, and they chose even. The wheel stopped at 11. As a result, Buffalo was given the first overall selection, which it used to choose Perreault. He scored 38 goals as a rookie and captured the Calder Trophy as rookie of the year. Previously, Imlach had handed off 11 to an incoming rookie for good luck, but even he knew not to mess with a good thing and Perreault kept the number for 17 years.

Gilbert Perreault

ANOTHER PERREAULT, YANIC, was a high-scoring centre in the Quebec Major Junior Hockey League (QMJHL) when he was drafted by the Toronto Maple Leafs in 1991. In junior and with the Leafs, Perreault wore 44 because his birth date is April 4 (fourth day of the fourth month). Perreault kept the number at subsequent stops in the league, but was forced to change when he signed on with the Montreal Canadiens as a free agent in 2001. In Montreal, 44 belonged to defenceman Sheldon Souray, so Perreault decided to adopt the unique number of his former Toronto line-mate Sergei Berezin and took 94. He called Berezin in the summer and asked if it would be all right for him to take the number. Berezin, who had also left the Leafs to join Phoenix, happily agreed. However, if Sergei had known what lay ahead, he might not have been so generous. Later that season, Phoenix and Montreal struck a deal and Berezin landed with the Canadiens. With his number now on Perreault's back, Sergei had to settle for 95.

Michel Petit

NOBODY HAS PLAYED for more teams than defence-man Michel Petit, who suited up with ten different franchises during his NHL career. Petit managed to wear seven different numbers during his years in the league, running the gamut from 7 all the way up to 95. By the time he wore 95 with the Tampa Bay Lightning in 1995, he had moved around so much that choosing the year as his sweater number was a good way to remind him where he was playing! Petit's extended tour through the league ended in Phoenix where he played his final NHL game in 1998 as a member of the Coyotes. He then bounced around in the minors and had a few stints in Germany before taking one last kick at the can. In the fall of 2001, Petit attempted an NHL comeback with the Pittsburgh Penguins, which would have been his 11th NHL franchise. Though a late training camp cut, Petit did manage to wear yet another new sweater number, 26, for his single exhibition game appearance.

ROBERT PETROVICKY was a first-round selection by the Hartford Whalers in the 1992 Entry Draft and made the leap to the NHL that same year. Petrovicky, who was a star in his native Slovakia, left a tragedy behind when he made the trip to North America. His mother had been killed by a drunk driver when she was 39, so Petrovicky honoured her memory by wearing that number on his back. He was able to get 39 only with Hartford, however, finding the number unavailable during stints in Dallas, St. Louis, Tampa Bay, and Long Island. But when he continued his career in Europe in 2000 or played for Slovakia in international games, he reverted to 39.

Keith Primeau

KEITH PRIMEAU, who spent time with Detroit and Hartford/Carolina before landing in the City of Brotherly Love, wore 55 during his first two NHL stops. "When I was a kid," he explained, "I used to wear number 5. One summer when I played hockey there was another kid who used to wear 5 in the winter so only one of us could have it. I lost the coin toss so my dad said, 'If you can't have 5, why don't you take 55?' and I have worn that ever since." That is, until he was traded to the Philadelphia Flyers, where Ulf Samuelsson wore 55 (ironically for the same reason that Primeau started wearing it—because 5 was unavailable). In search of a new number, Primeau decided to go with a "family" number, the same one his son wore in minor hockey. "The reason I have 25 now is because my oldest son, Corey, wears 25 because he takes one of Uncle Wayne's numbers, 22, and one of my numbers, 55, and combines them to make 25." Uncle Wayne is Keith's brother, also an NHLer. So, Keith's son wore a number to honour his dad and uncle, and then it all came full circle when the elder Primeau returned the favour and adopted his son's number.

Henri Richard

MANY HOCKEY PLAYERS, especially in Quebec, grew up wearing 9 because of the great Maurice "The Rocket" Richard. But few players can say that they didn't get to wear that number because Richard himself was their teammate. The only one who can make that claim is his brother, Henri Richard, who joined the Montreal Canadiens to start his NHL career in 1955. "I couldn't get 9. My brother Maurice was wearing that number. Because of my brother Maurice, I wore 9 in junior. Elmer Lach retired the year before I came up (1954) and he wore 16. That was the number they gave me. I couldn't speak English so I couldn't ask for any special number." In the end, 16 turned out to be a great fit for the player whom Canadiens fans would call "The Pocket Rocket." Richard played 20 seasons in Montreal, scored over 1,000 career points, and captured a league-record 11 Stanley Cups. When his career ended in 1975, the Canadiens retired his 16 and hoisted it to the rafters of the Montreal Forum where it hung next to his brother's famous 9.

HE WAS KNOWN as "The Rocket" during his Hall of Fame career with the Montreal Canadiens and cemented his place in hockey history when he scored 50 goals in 50 games during the 1944–45 season. The fiery Maurice Richard wore 15 during his rookie season with the Habs (1942–43), but after just 16 games he suffered a broken leg and missed the rest of the year. Just before the start of his second season in the NHL, Richard's wife gave birth to their first child, Huguette, who weighed nine pounds. The 9 had become available when Charlie Sands left the Habs to play in New York. Richard saw this as a sign and decided to change his number to 9. With the new digit on his back, he blossomed into a superstar, scoring a team-leading 32 goals to start a goal-scoring legacy that would see Richard's 9 retired and raised to the rafters of the Forum in Montreal. The Rocket's relationship with 9 was so strong that even decades after his retirement he included the number when he signed an autograph. Richard would sign his name, then add the circled 9. For Maurice Richard, 9 was part of his legacy.

MARTIN RUCINSKY FOUND himself caught in the NHL spotlight for the first time when he was included in the group of players sent to the Montreal Canadiens by Colorado in exchange for superstar Patrick Roy late in 1995. It was after that blockbuster trade that Rucinsky first got to wear 26 in the NHL. For Rucinsky, the number was always his first choice. "That was the number I got when I broke into the Czech league, playing professionally for the first time when I was 17." However, during his second stint in New York, he also joined a very exclusive sweater-number club. On November 1, 2003, at Montreal, Martin Rucinsky's 26 sweater was badly torn in the first period and had to be stitched up. Rather then have Rucinsky sit out waiting for his sweater to be repaired, the training staff simply got him one of the extra sweaters from the dressing room and he returned to action wearing a 41 with no nameplate. By the time the second period began, his original sweater had been repaired and he completed the game wearing 26. Rucinsky thus became just the second NHL player (after Theo Fleury) to wear two different sweater numbers in one game.

COLORADO AVALANCHE SUPERSTAR Joe Sakic has enjoyed so much success wearing 19 that few people can remember him ever wearing another number in the NHL. During his first season in the league, however, he wore the flashy 88 with the Quebec Nordiques (1988–89). Sakic had worn 19 during his highly successful junior career but when he arrived in Quebec for his first training camp he found that 19 belonged to defenceman Alain Cote. Because his rookie season was 1988, Sakic simply choose the year as his sweater number. When Cote retired in the summer of 1989, Sakic switched to 19, which he has worn ever since. However, he did run into a numbers quandary again in 1998. When Sakic joined Team Canada for the Nagano Olympics, his more senior teammate Steve Yzerman wore 19. Sakic opted to invert the digits and wore 91 at the tournament. In the summer of 2004, Sakic again represented his country at the World Cup of Hockey, and with Yzerman injured and unable to play, he was free to wear 19. Out of respect, he opted to stick with 91, calling it his "international number."

MATHIEU SCHNEIDER began his NHL career with the Montreal Canadiens in 1987 wearing 18. But when Hall of Famer Denis Savard was acquired by the Canadiens in 1990, Schneider surrendered the number, dropped the 1 from 18, and wore 8. But things didn't go well with the new number, and Schneider switched to 27. The Montreal Canadiens won the Stanley Cup, which Schneider saw as a sign that his luck had changed. However, when he was traded to the New York Islanders a season and a half later, Derek King already had 27, so Schneider inverted the number and wore 72. Shortly after, he was sent to the Toronto Maple Leafs and kept 72. On the eve of the 1998–99 season, he was traded yet again. It occurred to Schneider that the number was no longer bringing him luck, so when he joined the New York Rangers he selected 26. The next year, Schneider changed to 21. When he signed with the Los Angeles Kings in the summer of 2000, he moved on to 10. Late in the 2002–03 season, the Kings traded him to the Detroit Red Wings. Schneider settled on 23, his eighth number in the NHL.

18
8
27
72
26
21
10
23
5

Daniel & Henrik Sedin

FORMER VANCOUVER CANUCKS general manager Brian Burke stole the show at the 1999 NHL Entry Draft when his wheeling and dealing netted him the second and third overall picks, which he used to select the talented Sedin twins, Daniel and Henrik. The highly touted Swedish brothers arrived in the NHL in the fall of 2000 to join the Canucks, but both found the sweater numbers from their time in Sweden unavailable with Vancouver. Henrik wore 20 and Daniel 12 during their time with MoDo of the Swedish Elite League, but with both numbers taken, the Canucks came up with a clever alternative. Daniel, who was selected second overall in the draft, would wear 22, and his brother, who was drafted third, would wear 33. Since they are identical twins, fans can remember now which brother was drafted higher, based on sweater numbers.

Eddie Shack

KNOWN AS "THE ENTERTAINER" because of his high energy, Eddie Shack played with a reckless style during a lengthy career that saw him suit up for six teams, including two memorable stints with the Toronto Maple Leafs. Growing up, Shack always wore 23 and kept that number during all but one of his NHL stops. When he began his NHL career with the New York Rangers, he was disappointed to find 23 taken, so he had to settle for 5 and later 6. However, a trade to the Leafs not only energized Shack's career, but also allowed him to wear 23. He continued to do so during stops in Boston, Los Angeles, and Buffalo. In 1972, Shack joined the Pittsburgh Penguins and once again found his 23 taken, so he played with 24 for one season. When the player who had his number, Bob Leiter, was claimed by the Atlanta Flames in the Expansion Draft, Shack reclaimed his 23. Shack ended his career back in Toronto, where he had enjoyed his best seasons, and retired wearing his beloved 23. But why did Shack have such an attachment to the digits? The reason was simple: Shack's initials, E.S., written backward, resemble number 23.

Neil Sheehy

NEIL SHEEHY SPENT nine seasons in the NHL with three different clubs. The defenceman began his career with the Calgary Flames in 1983, where he wore 5. During the 1987–88 season, his fifth with Calgary, Sheehy was traded to the Hartford Whalers, where he was unable to wear 5 because it belonged to Ulf Samuelsson. In need of a new number, Sheehy opted for the highly unusual 0. He joked that he chose 0 because of one of his former "Battle of Alberta" foes, Wayne Gretzky. "Zero is the furthest away from 99, and talent-wise, I was as far away from 99 as possible." But the real reason was much more personal. Sheehy explains, "When my grandparents came to the United States from Ireland, our family name was O'Sheehy. I wore zero to get the 'O' back." So for that one season, on the back of his sweater, he was "O'Sheehy" once again. Years later, the NHL implemented a rule regarding sweater numbers that banned the use of 0 or 00, so Sheehy will go down in history as the NHL's last 0.

Darryl Sittler

WHEN THE MAPLE LEAFS drafted Darryl Sittler in 1970, they felt they were getting someone special. Accordingly, they assigned the young centre 27. The 27 had strong ties with Maple Leaf fans because for more than 11 years it belonged to fan favourite Frank Mahovlich. But "Big M's" departure in March 1968 had not been amicable, so the Leafs wanted to put the number back in circulation as quickly as possible. Sittler recalls how he discovered he would be wearing sweater 27. "I had never been in Maple Leaf Gardens before and I was with [former Leafs executive] Jim Gregory. We walked into the Leafs dressing room and he pointed at a locker over toward the corner. 'You'll be over there,' he said. The sweater was hanging there. Number 27. I knew what that meant." Sittler would do the number proud, leading the Maple Leafs in scoring for seven straight seasons and eventually wearing the captain's "C" in Toronto. When the Maple Leafs announced their All-Time Dream Team, Sittler was voted as the number-one centreman. On the left wing, fittingly, the fans voted Frank Mahovlich.

Martin Skoula

DEFENCEMAN MARTIN SKOULA wore 55 in his rookie season with the Colorado Avalanche, the number he was issued in training camp. When he returned for his second season in the NHL with the Avs in 2000–01, he was sporting a new, more unusual number. Skoula began the season wearing 41, which seemed an odd choice. It turns out Skoula wore 14 as a junior, but that number was assigned to Dave Reid so Skoula inverted the digits and wore 41. When Reid left the team, Skoula decided not to flip to 14 because he had won the Stanley Cup wearing 41 and didn't want to change his luck. When Skoula was traded to the Mighty Ducks of Anaheim during the 2003–04 season, he finally settled on his first choice and wore 14.

Ryan Smyth

RYAN SMYTH IS A TOUGH, skilled winger with the Edmonton Oilers who has not only shone at the NHL level but also helped Team Canada capture a gold medal at the 2002 Olympic Winter Games and the 2003 and 2004 World Championships. Smyth wears the unusual 94 on his sweater. Though it might be an uncommon number in the NHL, his reason for choosing it is personal. When he was growing up, Smyth's dream of a career in the NHL was not always nurtured by those around him. As he struggled to balance hockey and school, he was often told he was wasting his time and that the NHL was an unachievable goal. With his mind so focused on hockey, his grades slipped, until it seemed that graduating from high school would be another tough hurdle to clear. In 1994, Smyth reached two major milestones: he did, indeed, graduate, and he also became a first-round draft pick of the Edmonton Oilers. Now, when Smyth skates on the NHL or on international ice, he does so with 94 on his back, a constant reminder to all who doubted him. Smyth proved that if you work hard enough and believe in your dreams, you can achieve whatever you set your mind on.

Jason Spezza

JASON SPEZZA'S FIRST CHOICE for a sweater number is the classic 9. When 9 isn't available, as was the case during his junior stints in Mississauga, Windsor, and Belleville, Spezza improvises. In Mississauga, he took 19, and during his next two stops he doubled nine and wore 18. When Spezza made the leap to the NHL with the Ottawa Senators in 2002–03, he found that 9 belonged to winger Martin Havlat. The 18 wasn't available and neither was 19. Spezza needed to find a number with 9 in it, so he settled on 39. "I didn't have a lot of choice," he recalled. "I like nines. I've worn 9, 18. . . . I could have had 27, which is a multiple of nine, but I just kind of went with this." During the 2003–04 season, Senators forward Peter Schastlivy was traded to the Mighty Ducks of Anaheim, which freed up 19 in the Senators dressing room. Spezza was quick to pounce on it and move closer to his coveted 9. Though he still hasn't arrived at his first-choice number in Ottawa, he did get to wear 9 with the Senators' farm club. During the hockey lockout of 2004–05, Spezza was loaned to the team's affiliate in Binghamton where he dazzled the American Hockey League (AHL) while wearing his coveted 9, a year in which he was named the league's MVP.

Peter Stastny

THE SECOND OF THREE Stastny brothers, Peter was a dominant offensive force, one of the NHL's first European superstars, and the man responsible for putting the Quebec Nordiques on the NHL map. Stastny, who played on a line with his two brothers while in Quebec, wore 18 with his club team back home in the former Czechoslovakia. However, when he joined the Czech national team, 18 was unavailable. The Czech custom was that a player simply took the next highest number available, which in this case turned out to be 26. When he made the jump to the NHL, he took his now-familiar 26. In the late 1980s, the Nordiques began to struggle. Stastny was traded to the New Jersey Devils in 1990, but the trade forced more than just a change of location. Stastny discovered that defenceman Tommy Albelin had 26 and so, following the Czech custom, Stastny took 29, which was the next available number. The change didn't last long, however, because Albelin soon surrendered 26 to Stastny out of respect.

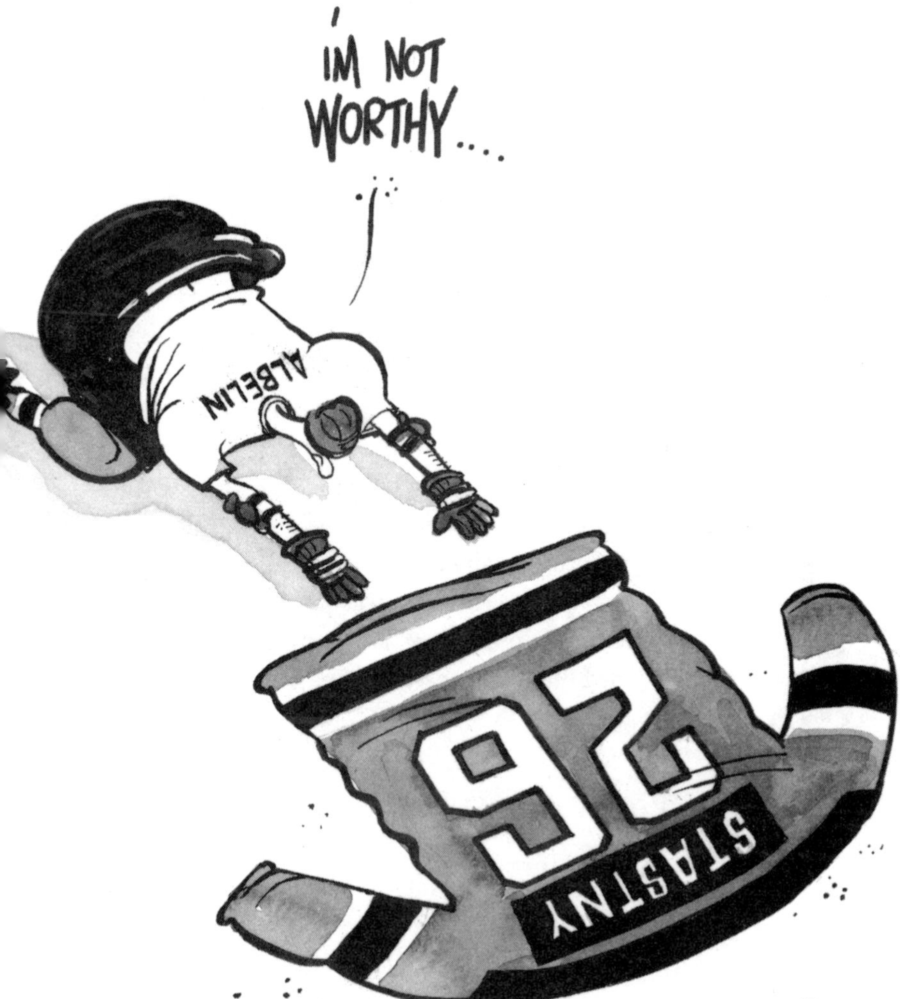
I'M NOT WORTHY....
ALBELIN
26
STASTNY

Martin St. Louis

MARTIN ST. LOUIS WENT from being an undrafted forward to leading the NHL in scoring and capturing the Stanley Cup with the Tampa Bay Lightning in 2003–04. The diminutive star wore 8 at the University of Vermont and took 15 when he made his NHL debut with the Calgary Flames in 1998. But when he signed on with the Lightning he switched numbers. In Tampa Bay, St. Louis adopted 26 because it belonged to his childhood hero, former Montreal Canadiens star Mats Naslund. St. Louis, who stands 5'8", but is still a dominant scorer because of his skill and shiftiness, had a great role model in Naslund. The former Swedish national team hero was just 5'7" but still developed into an offensive leader for the Canadiens and helped them win the 1986 Stanley Cup.

CENTRE MATS SUNDIN became the first Swedish-born player to be selected first overall in the NHL Entry Draft when the Quebec Nordiques selected him in 1989. He became the first player in the history of the organization to wear "unlucky" 13. In his case, luck—good or bad—wasn't part of his decision. Simply, Sundin's birthday is February 13.

Alex Tanguay

COLORADO AVALANCHE sniper Alex Tanguay wore 40, a number he was given at his first Avalanche camp and which he was wearing when the team won the Stanley Cup in 2001. The following season, with a championship ring on his finger, he felt like an established NHLer and intended to switch numbers. His plan was to switch to 18, which had become available because of the trade of Adam Deadmarsh in February 2001. But that plan soon hit a snag. One of Tanguay's young teammates, Chris Drury, also had designs on the number. Drury, who had seniority over Tanguay (by just one season), made the move first and switched from 37 to 18. Unable to get the number, Tanguay decided to keep 40, in part because he had seen many fans wearing 40 sweaters in the crowd and didn't want to make their sweaters obsolete. In 2003, however, Drury was traded to Buffalo and 18 became available again. Tanguay seized the opportunity and officially switched. The new number seemed to suit him, as he scored 25 goals and a career-best 79 points in just 69 games for the Avalanche in the 2003–04 season.

JOSE THEODORE JOINED a long list of great Montreal
Canadiens goaltenders to win a major NHL award
when he captured the Vezina Trophy and Hart Trophy
in 2001–02. When Theodore first played for the
Canadiens in 1995–96, he wore 37, but after just
one game he was sent back to the minors. When he
returned to the NHL the following season, 37 was
being worn by Tomas Vokoun, so he had to choose
a new number. As a student in Vladislav Tretiak's goaltending school during the off-season, Theodore had
long planned to wear 20 as a tribute to his mentor.
However, earlier that same year the Chicago
Blackhawks had traded Ed Belfour to the San Jose
Sharks. Belfour, a protégé of Tretiak, had decided to
wear 20, so Theodore, feeling that he had been beaten
to the punch, searched for a new number. Lacking
any of his own ideas, Theodore turned to the team
equipment manager, who suggested he take 60 because
no goalie had ever worn that number. Theodore did.

THE HULKING JOE THORNTON was the first overall pick of the Boston Bruins in the 1997 NHL Entry Draft. The skilled forward was touted by many scouts as a franchise player because of his combination of skill and size. Thornton, however, admired a different style of player. He had worn 19 with the Soo Greyhounds during his junior career in the Ontario Hockey League (OHL) and wanted to continue wearing that number with the Bruins because his older brother's favourite player was Detroit Red Wings captain Steve Yzerman. However, checking forward Rob DiMaio was already wearing 19 for Boston. At the urging of his agent, Thornton decided to look for an unusual number that he could make his own. He decided on 6, perhaps the least popular of the single-digit numbers. The idea was that Thornton could be the definitive 6. The plan didn't exactly play out that way, however. Thornton spent three seasons wearing 6, but when DiMaio left the club in 2000, "Big Joe" made the switch to 19 and blossomed into one of the game's top forwards.

WHEN RICK TOCCHET first made it to the NHL with Philadelphia in 1984, he selected 22 and wore it until his trade to Pittsburgh in 1992. In Pittsburgh, Paul Stanton wore 22, so Tocchet adopted the year as his sweater number and took 92. The Penguins won the Stanley Cup that spring. When Stanton was traded to the Boston Bruins, Tocchet adopted 22. After parts of three seasons with the Penguins, Tocchet was traded to the Los Angeles Kings and found that 22 belonged to Charlie Huddy. He went back to 92 until Huddy was dealt to the Sabres and Tocchet took 22. In 1996, after 80 games with the Kings, Tocchet moved to the Boston Bruins, where 22 was being worn by Jozef Stumpel. Rookie Stumpel deferred to the veteran Tocchet and gave up the number. After a brief stop in Washington wearing 92, Tocchet joined the Phoenix Coyotes where veteran Mike Gartner wore 22, so the player went with his backup 92. The pattern continued when Gartner retired and Tocchet switched to 22. Eventually he was sent back to the Flyers to find defenceman Luke Richardson now had 22, so Tocchet wore 92. Tocchet is the only player to wear the same two numbers with four different teams.

RICK VAIVE WAS ASSIGNED 22 while in junior and by the time he broke into the NHL with the Vancouver Canucks, he had grown attached to the number and wanted to continue wearing it. Bob Manno wore 22 with the Canucks and Vaive was given 18 instead. Vaive didn't wear that number for very long. Shortly after his rookie season began, a high school friend contacted him and urged him to switch to a higher number because he felt that 18 was bad luck. A mutual friend, their high school's star quarterback who wore 18, had recently been killed in a car accident. The friend believed 18 was now bad luck. Vaive agreed, switched to 28, and was shortly traded to the Toronto Maple Leafs. One of the players he was traded for, Dave "Tiger" Williams, wore 22 for the Blue and White, but management felt that because Williams was one of the city's most popular athletes, it would be unwise to give the new acquisition Williams' number. Instead, Vaive was given 20, but after just a few games decided it was more important to have his favourite 22 than to worry about the inevitable comparisons to the Tiger. Thus, Vaive wore four sweater numbers with two teams over the course of his rookie season.

AARON WARD played only sporadically for six years in Detroit, but he managed to wear six different sweater numbers. During his first training camp with the Wings, he wore 61. When he made the team, he was given 29. That lasted just five games before he was asked to surrender the number when the Red Wings acquired veteran goaltender Mike Vernon in the summer of 1994. Ward then took 8 but that number was given to Igor Larionov when the Russian joined Detroit early in the 1995–96 season. Next, Ward took 14, but yet again, the Red Wings made a big trade for a high-profile player and Ward's number was given to Brendan Shanahan when Shanahan arrived in October 1996. Ward settled on 27, and when he finally began to establish himself as a regular member of the Red Wings defence, he thought his days of number swapping were done. However, during a road trip to Buffalo, Ward arrived at the rink to find 39 hanging in his stall instead of 27. The Red Wing training staff had forgotten to pack his road sweater, so Ward took to the ice with his sixth different number. After his trade to Carolina, Ward took yet another number—4.

Harry Watson

IN THE POST-WAR YEARS, Hall of Fame left winger Harry Watson wore 4 during his time with the Toronto Maple Leafs, a rather unusual number for a forward. The number is usually reserved for a defenceman and it was for that reason that Watson was originally assigned the number. Maple Leafs owner Conn Smythe thought Watson would make a great defenceman because of his size and strength. On his first day of training camp with the team, Watson played defence. During one scrimmage, Leafs star Syl Apps went around Watson with ease and scored a goal. Smythe was incensed. He bellowed at Watson to get back to playing forward and the short-lived experiment was over, but the number remained on his back. Smythe's next idea for Watson was much more fruitful. He placed him on the wing with Apps at centre and the line became the offensive force that won four Stanley Cup titles in Watson's nine years with the team (1946–55).

NEW YORK RANGERS netminder Kevin Weekes wears 80 as a result of a little-known league rule. In the late 1990s, the NHL switched to a new software system to track league statistics, resulting in a rule change for sweater numbers. The program tracked each player in the league by his sweater number, but the system did not recognize 0, so, as a result, the league forbade the use of 0 or 00 for its players. Weekes wanted to wear 00, so he chose 80 instead because he felt that it looked the closest to the digits. Weekes tried different numbers during stops in Florida, Vancouver, and Long Island, but after joining the Tampa Bay Lightning he settled on 80, which he also wore in Carolina and will likely continue to wear with the Rangers with whom he signed as a free agent in August 2004.

KYLE WELLWOOD WAS a fifth-round draft pick of the Toronto Maple Leafs in 2001 and made his debut with the club during the 2003–04 season. For that game, he wore the unfamiliar 42. During his junior career and with the Leafs farm club in St. John's, Wellwood wore 97. He chose the unusual number because of family ties. His grandfather was a big Detroit Red Wings fan and his two favourite players were Gordie Howe and Ted Lindsay. Howe wore 9 and Lindsay wore 7, so the youngster put both numbers on his back as a nod to his grandfather. It's safe to say that when Wellwood made his big league debut, he quickly supplanted Howe and Lindsay in the eyes of his grandfather and became his new favourite NHL player.

Dave "Tiger" Williams

DAVE "TIGER" WILLIAMS was one of the premier tough guys in the NHL in the 1970s and '80s, becoming a fan favourite not only for his pugilistic prowess but also for his colourful goal celebrations. Tiger split his first ten seasons in the NHL between the Toronto Maple Leafs and the Vancouver Canucks, establishing himself as a feared fighter and a decent scorer, scoring 35 goals in the 1980–81 season. After five years in Vancouver, Williams joined the Detroit Red Wings prior to the start of the 1984–85 season. When he arrived in Motown, the 22 that he wore in Toronto and Vancouver belonged to veteran defenceman Brad Park. Tiger selected 55 because it looked like an upside-down 22. Williams struggled in Detroit, scoring just three goals in, ironically, 55 games, and spent time in the minor leagues. Eventually he joined the Los Angeles Kings, where he was able to wear his preferred 22 again. With his familiar number on his back, Williams rebounded and scored 20 goals in his first full season in L.A.

AT 6'6", PETER WORRELL immediately became a recognizable presence in the NHL. The tough-guy winger soon built a reputation as one of the league's most feared fighters. Growing up, Worrell was a big fan of Bruins forward Cam Neely and always wore his 8 when he got the chance. When he began his NHL career with Florida in 1997, Worrell's favourite number was unavailable so he settled for 28 and two seasons later he switched to 8. After six years with the Panthers, Worrell was traded to the Colorado Avalanche where another new addition, Teemu Selanne, wore 8. Worrell needed to find a new number and opted for 28 again, keeping the 8 in his number so he could continue to acknowledge Cam Neely.

THE NUMBER 19 HAD A LONG and undistinguished history in Detroit before rookie centre Steve Yzerman selected it as his sweater number in 1983. He became the 62nd player to wear that number with the Red Wings, but his incredible career with the club guarantees he will also be the last. Yzerman didn't always wear 19. When he moved to Ontario from B.C. as a ten-year-old and joined the Nepean Raiders, Yzerman wore 14. A few years later, while in summer hockey camp, he decided to switch to 19 because of his admiration for New York Islanders star Bryan Trottier. Over his long, successful career in Motown, Yzerman and his 19 have become so iconic that when an injury forced him to miss the 2004 World Cup of Hockey, no player on the team wore 19 despite the fact that four among them wore the number with their NHL teams. Shane Doan of Phoenix (9), Joe Sakic of Colorado (91), Joe Thornton of Boston (97), and Brad Richards of Tampa Bay (39) all selected different numbers out of respect to Yzerman.

Acknowledgements

The authors would like to thank the many people who have done their best to make this book possible: publisher Jordan Fenn, for his continued support; editor Janie Yoon and art director Peter Maher for their enthusiasm; Tony Jenkins for bringing his skills and imagination to the drafting table and creating wonderful caricatures. We would also like to thank Steve Poirier and Kevin Shea at the Hockey Hall of Fame for gathering stories when they could, and Mike Bolt, for picking up stories while trailing the Stanley Cup around the world.

Andrew Podnieks would particularly like to thank his family—Liz, Ian, Zack, Emily, and mom—as well as a few friends who contributed nothing to these stories but whose insanity kept him able-minded to write them, notably Jon and Joan Redfern, Cathy Gildiner, and the amazing Mary Jane Nguyen, doctor, photographer, philosopher.

Rob Hynes would like to thank his wife, Andrea, for her undying enthusiasm and support, and his mother and father for paying for the expensive goaltending equipment that he wore growing up. Finally, a thank you goes out to the only number ten that really mattered, Guy Lafleur—the first number Rob had to have stitched on the back of a sweater, and the person responsible for a lifelong fascination with who wore what and why.

Andrew Podnieks is the best-selling author of more than 20 books on hockey, most recently *The Sensational Sidney Crosby; Silverware; Lord Stanley's Cup; The Flames: Celebrating Calgary's Dream Season 2003–04; Players: The Ultimate A–Z Guide of Everyone Who Has Played in the NHL;* and *A Day in the Life of the Maple Leafs*. Podnieks has worn #6 all his life in tribute to Ace Bailey, whose daughter, Joyce, took him to his first Leafs game many years ago. For more information on Andrew Podnieks, please visit his website at www.andrewpodnieks.com.

Rob Hynes is a freelance writer whose lifelong interest in sweater numbers began when he received a Guy Lafleur #10 Canadiens sweater as a Christmas present in 1984. Since then, he's tracked who wore what and why, while working for the Hockey Hall of Fame and Rogers Sportsnet. Hynes, a goaltender, wore #37 early on as a tribute to Steve Penney. He later settled on #32, which he has proudly worn with an assortment of teams over the last 15 seasons. Unfortunately, for somebody so intrigued by the stories behind the numbers, he wears #32 only because he likes the way it looks.

Anthony Jenkins joined *The Globe and Mail* in 1974, where for over three decades he has drawn editorial cartoons, caricatures, and illustrations. During the 1980s, he also began writing for the paper. Jenkins has been playing pick-up hockey with the same core group of players (both men and women) for the last 27 seasons. He wears #50, his age when the sweater was given to him, and the name "Big Skate" (a disparaging reference to alleged lethargic looping turns) appears on his Brampton Batallion warm-up jersey. Jenkins lives in Toronto with his wife and two daughters. For more information on Anthony Jenkins, please visit www.jenkinsdraws.com.